Te

Dr. Shelly Senders

On May 25, 2009, Lorelle Pride was delivered gently into this world by Cesarean section. She was named Lorelle, which in Latin means *little laurel tree*. The laurel tree is a prominent symbol of victory, as its branches are used to create crowns and wreaths for winning athletes. There is a beautiful Jewish tradition and belief that the only forms of prophecy that still exist are the names that parents give to their children. And Lorelle was certainly a winner.

Diagnosed with what was termed an incurable genetic disease, her parents were told she might not even make it into this world. But Lorelle and her parents ignored the textbook and defied the odds. And every day of her 6.5 years, she fought, and she smiled. For a time, she owned the record for the number of heart-rate drops in the ICU. But they never seemed to bother her. And each time she was resuscitated, each time she came off the ventilator, she smiled so effusively that it was impossible not to appreciate that she was sent to this world as a blessing, for those of us who came into her orbit to gain a greater appreciation for the physical world around us and for the people who inhabit that world. In her short life, Lorelle brought a lifetime of happiness to her family, friends, medical providers, and anyone privileged to know her. The Lorelle

Faith Pride Foundation is a testament to Lorelle's continued impact on the world.

And this book of devotional and inspirational readings is another gift to those who were not privileged to know Lorelle personally. Her mother, Kodi Pride, has transformed her grief into prayer, her sadness into a dialogue with God, and her personal loss into a victory for humanity. Lorelle may mean *little laurel tree* in Latin, and she may have served as a symbol of that victory. But in Hebrew, Lorelle means *by the Light of God*.

May this devotional book of writings serve as a light forward for all who read it, and may it help them gain a greater spiritual connection with God. May it help transform lives beset by anxiety, depression, and sadness into ones full of anticipation, hope, and happiness. And may Lorelle's trademark smile that hovers over this book bring out a similar smile in all who are fortunate enough to be inspired by its pages.

The
Bereaved
Believer

The Same God of My Salvation and My Sorrow

Kodi B. Pride

ISBN 979-8-218-95787-2

First Edition, February 2023
Printed in the United States of America
Case #: 1-12143124162

Halo Publishing International is a self-publishing company that publishes adult fiction and non-fiction, children's literature, self-help, spiritual, and faith-based books. We continually strive to help authors reach their publishing goals and provide many different services that help them do so. We do not publish books that are deemed to be politically, religiously, or socially disrespectful, or books that are sexually provocative, including erotica. Halo reserves the right to refuse publication of any manuscript if it is deemed not to be in line with our principles. Do you have a book idea you would like us to consider publishing? Please visit www.halopublishing.com for more information.

LEGACY REMAINS

In celebration of her life and legacy.

If we never get an answer, why? We are encouraged that God still hears our cries. We dedicate this book to Lorelle Faith Pride, our glimpse of God's heartbeat here on Earth!

Lorelle Faith was a living miracle that changed our world; to us, she was the perfect little girl. Her life, light, and smile exemplified the Lord's joy, and we pray that her legacy will always show God glorified. In 2,373 days, Lorelle's life forever changed our yesterdays, today, and tomorrows, and her beautiful spirit lives on even in our sorrow. It is by faith that she lived and by faith that we find grace in grief.

May our angel rest peacefully in the grace of God, and may we all live a life that will be remembered and not just numbered.

Lorelle Faith Pride
May 25, 2009–November 23, 2015

CONTENTS

FOREWORD BY
CHRISTI TRIPODI

A ll of us belong to a club we never wanted to be a part of, yet this bereaved believer is a witness of the great hope we all have in our Lord and Savior Jesus Christ. To know we will see our loved ones again is a great reason to get out of bed each morning. God did not promise us an easy life, but He did promise us an eternal life!!!

This devotional is not just words on a page; these are lived by Kodi Pride ONLY BECAUSE SHE HAS LOVED SO DEEPLY AND LOST SO DEEPLY HER PRECIOUS DAUGHTER, LORELLE. We were not meant to walk this journey alone; Kodi's prayerful reflections will provide the necessary companion for you as you unite your sufferings with Christ. We are in this together, dear friends; my prayer is that you never grieve alone.

DEAR READER,

Do I have all the answers? No, grief is often collectively felt, yet individually processed. This devotional has no specific dates or days because I realized that what I need changes, often daily. I give myself the freedom to return to a page. Grief is a constant process with no page order.

I chose to write a devotional because, in grief, I found sometimes I could only ingest small doses of words and insight. Sometimes too much of anything overwhelmed my heart, mind, and soul. Yet, in small mustard-seed moments, I could retain inspiration and remain encouraged. From this space of reflection, I share personal meditations during my bereavement. Daily I wrote with transparency and a capacity for bearing an unwavering truth; I can only pour out from what has been poured within.

Now, I am not a grief counselor, but I am someone who has lost and lived. I am a mother who got inducted into a sorority of bereaved mothers without choice. I have studied, accepted therapy, and sought the face and hand of God when death appealed as the only rest I could find. I am someone who believes that the testimonies of others encourage others. I am someone who knows that, in loss, you can gain. I am someone who knew a lot but nothing about the pain I was experiencing.

Spiritually, my daughter lost her earthly body but gained eternal life. Physically, I lost my daughter, whom I carried in my arms, and now I carry in my heart. Holistically, what I gained was a truth that suffocates my human feelings. Biblically, I know God is near to the brokenhearted and those crushed in spirit; I know He is the lifter of my head; I know He is unfailing in His everlasting love for His children. I know that weeping endures for a night, but joy comes in the morning. Gratefully, I do not know how long the night is, but I know His joy came in my morning and mourning. Honestly, I am not a grief expert, only a partaker.

On November 23, 2015, I lost my favorite patient, my youngest daughter, the one I would have exchanged my life for if given the option. I lost everything I knew as normal, but not my faith. I accepted death as an end, but it was an immediate beginning to a life-changing journey I must travel. I remember having the most difficulty closing her little casket, but I felt her saying, *"Mommy, live. I am resting."*

Truthfully, I wanted to DIE, but I heard God question me, *"Don't you want the life I am giving you? Who will tell her story if you die?"* So I decided to live the life my daughter had never experienced. I realized her purpose remained beyond her remains. So with her legacy in spirit, I chose to survive and thrive.

Like many mourners, I have days that I merely exist with a broken heart, crushed hope, and fragile praise. But, daily, the sufficiency of God's grace allows me to live and not just be alive. I thought grief only rested on you, but I learned it is something that embeds within you. In my sorrow, I found a secret and sacred place in God. Yes, in the grief, not through it or after it, but right in the thick of it, I experienced God like never before.

I pray this devotion illuminates how beautifully God rests His sufficient grace in grief.

Sincerely,
Kodi

ABSENT...YET SO PRESENT

B*reathe, breathe,* is what I tell myself every day; God has a purpose and a plan, despite my sorrow. The death of my child snatched the breath from my lungs. For the first time in my life, I felt unable to exhale. I lost my breath, but somehow gained faith. This devastating loss catapulted my FAITH into a permanent place. I began a relentless pursuit, always to seek God's peace. Sorrow had become heavy, causing me to rely on God and rest in HIS WILL. In this space, I hold on to the fact He is the God who can make the storm be still. With God, I found restoration and safety. Yet it was through the life and death of Lorelle FAITH that I experienced the comfort of the Holy Spirit.

To my daughter, I thank you for living in my heart. You fought to the last heartbeat, and I owe you the same tenacity. As a believer, my faith has been intensely tested. But God's grace is sufficient in ALL things, and my sorrow was a part of the ALL. I pray I always remember my story with Lorelle, when I saw the SON shine!

NOW, TAKE A MOMENT AND BREATHE;
LET YOUR LOVED ONE'S MEMORY
BE FULL OF LIGHT AND LOVE.

We are confident, yes, well pleased rather to be
absent from the body and to be present with the Lord.
(2 Corinthians 5:8, New King James Version)

Now Faith

F rankly, grief has changed and infused my faith in ways I can barely articulate.

Grief has become part of me in a capacity I did not realize I could be filled. I had an invisible void that appeared when death became a reality. There was a naïve and natural part of my heart that was deepened in loss, yet submerged in love. My daughter's passing left me with a yearning that was only subdued by memories.

Memories bring up several emotions; it takes faith to remember and reflect. It takes "now faith" to endure your loss. Faith that you can access at any moment empowers you to press past your pain. You may feel as if you will drown in your sorrows, but you can make it. Your faith is not in you; it is in God. God does not fail, so redirect your faith in His process. So when grief comes in as if the floodgates have burst, let faith be a raft to keep you afloat.

YOUR FAITH WILL NOT FAIL YOU.

Now faith is the substance of things hoped for, the evidence of things not seen. (Hebrews 11:1)

No Days Off

C an you miss a loved one every single day? Yes, you can, and, yes, I do! Every single, solitary day, there is a raw reality that my daughter has passed. Sometimes it feels similar to an unpleasant and unwanted dream. Envisioning living the rest of my life without my child feels incomprehensible. Yet what is inconceivable for me was permissible for God. God already made provision for this pain. God gave us a promised peace not predicated on our understanding.

Unfortunately, grief does not take a day off because you have an important meeting, a vacation, or a holiday. It is an uninvited guest that interrupts any experience or event without permission. However, there is still good news! God does not slumber or sleep. The Lord can provide hope, joy, comfort, or peace every day without delay.

EVERY DAY IS ANOTHER DAY, AND
I AM BLESSED TO REMEMBER YOU!

And God is able to make all grace abound toward you, that you, always having all sufficiency in all things, may have an abundance for every good work. (2 Corinthians 9:8)

In Weakness

I am not strong; I am weak, so weak that God had to become my sole strength. I am not always okay, but I remain assured that, someday, God will make a way. I am not beyond hurting; I am healing. I am not beyond grieving; I am striving to find purpose in pain. I am not existing; I am living. I am not stopping; I am moving through every hill and valley of this life journey. I am not beyond disappointment; I am just aware that my assignment in life is more significant than my emotions. I am not just a mom who lost a child; I am a woman who lives with a heart with an invisible hole. I am not just a woman who has had tough times; I am a person who still believes in the good of humanity. I am not just a person who has fallen; I am a Christian who, through Christ, rises back up. I am all that I am because of the GREAT I AM.

Have you ever experienced times that shook you to your very core?

WEAKNESS IS REIMAGINED AS A STRENGTH
TO LET GOD FIGHT MY BATTLES.

Then he said to them, "Go your way, eat the fat, drink
the sweet, and send portions to those for whom nothing is
prepared; for this day is holy to our Lord. Do not sorrow,
for the joy of the Lord is your strength." (Nehemiah 8:10)

CONSISTENT IN CRISIS

D id you know that when everything changes, God remains the same? He is the same Magnificent God to the whole and the broken. The same Present God to the glad and the sad. The same Compassionate God to the bereaved and the relieved. The same Just God to the wealthy and the poor. The same Powerful God to the striving and the struggling. The same Rescuing God to the fortified and the survived.

There is not one person, not one situation, not one pain, not one joy, not one purpose, not one circumstance for which God could not or would not SHOW UP. So, please, no matter your state, remain anchored in the FAITH. FAITH is a journey full of lessons and blessings. FAITH over Fear, Grace over Grief, Hope over Hopelessness. God is over everything! You shall—we shall—be Healed!

I'M APPEARING CRUSHED IN CHALLENGES, WHILE REALLY I'M BEING BUILT IN BELIEF.

Therefore you now have sorrow; but I will see you again, and your heart will rejoice, and your joy no one will take from you. (John 16:22)

CANDIDLY

How kind of God to give me time. How Kind of God to let His light Shine. How Kind of God to impose His Will beyond Mine. How Kind of God to consider me. How Kind of God to hear my plea. How Kind of God to take my tears and exchange them with triumph. To exchange my sorrow and give me Joy for tomorrow! To keep me in peace that surpasses understanding, even when my cares in life seem so demanding.

Oh, How Kind of God to reach down and rescue me, to not cast out, but pour out so I could see! How Kind of God to look beyond my faults and provide for my needs. God was present even when I was too busy to fall to my knees. How Kind of God to give me a chance to carry and bury a miracle so pure, then give me love to endure. Oh, How Kind of God to breathe upon me once again, to know when you think it is over, in Him it just begins. OH, HOW KIND OF GOD!

If you know God has been KIND to you, take a moment to think of HIS grace, mercy, and kindness.

GRATEFUL IN GRIEF AND THANKFUL IN TRIALS.

And be kind to one another, tenderhearted,
forgiving one another, even as God in Christ
forgave you. (Ephesians 4:32)

SUFFICIENT SYMPATHY

My typical reply is, "My sincere condolences, my sincere prayers. I am so sorry for your loss." I never claim to empathize with someone's loss because the emotions and processes of grief are unique. However, I deeply sympathize that suffering can be universally relatable; therefore, prayer is vital. Prayer can penetrate emotions personally experienced but holistically felt.

Today, I pray for those who grieve, that we do not get lost in the loss. I pray we can live with a broken heart, rejoice with a weeping soul, and heal with hope. When you lose someone you love, hurt is a feeling that only the Holy Spirit can comfort. In His divine and reserved comfort, we can journey through life with grace in grief.

CONDOLENCES ARE RECEIVED
WHERE HIS COMFORT RESIDES.

And He said to me, "My grace is sufficient for you, for My strength is made perfect in weakness." Therefore most gladly I will rather boast in my infirmities, that the power of Christ may rest upon me. (2 Corinthians 12:9)

Do Not Edit

Someone is barely holding on. Someone's stuck in a memory and a moment. Someone is unable to process pain. Someone is ready to give up. Someone is hurting deeply. Someone might be your family member or friend. Someone might be you in the mirror.

I know it is hard to support others when sometimes getting out of bed is challenging. However, I want to encourage you to press through your sorrow! You can show up for someone and yourself. How? You can pray. Do not give up on your loved ones who remain. Your prayers can reach where your presence cannot!

I am praying for parents who are grieving for children living and those who have passed. We forget some parents feel as if they have lost their children to drugs, alcoholism, violence, negative influences, mental illnesses, and physical diseases—and loss goes on and on. Then some parents have lost their children to death. I encourage all parents to hold on to hope that their children will be protected, and hold on to hope that they will see their children again.

Sometimes we parents shame ourselves too much. Try to do your best, and trust God to do the rest. Remember, your role in the script is a parent. The Author and the Finisher of our FAITH is the one who knows the whole story. We put our trust in God, Who wrote the book, not just a chapter.

YOUR ROLE AS A PARENT REMAINS IN GRIEF TOO!

For God so loved the world that He gave His only begotten Son, that whoever believes in Him should not perish but have everlasting life. (John 3:16)

VALLEY VOWS

I NEVER THOUGHT I WOULD MISS MY VALLEY SEASON UNTIL I REALIZED THE VALLEY WAS NOT MY POSITION; IT WAS MY STATE OF MIND. Lorelle's life shifted my valley mindset. I remember many days and nights I asked God how long my daughter would go through ups and downs, seizures, and surgeries.

Everything she endured, I also endured. As her mother, caregiver, and advocate, I wanted to carry the cross and take on the sickness and disorder, but it was not mine. Instead, I held her in a hopeful womb, a loving heart, a faithful spirit of faith, and a peaceful home. I often thought I would die witnessing her journey, but I was inspired and fortified. I was in a valley of trials and tribulations with a God-sent little angel named Lorelle Faith. Lorelle could not talk, but her life spoke to everyone who met her. She was the teacher of how to live, no matter what happens in life. Live life each day to the fullest.

I LEARNED THAT WHEN I LOOKED AROUND, THERE WAS VICTORY IN THE VALLEY! THE BEAUTY OF THE VALLEY IS IT IS A PERFECT PLACE TO LOOK UP. I LEARNED TO LOOK TO THE HILLS, FROM WHICH COMES ALL MY HELP, FOR MY HELP COMES FROM THE LORD!

I VOW TO REMAIN VICTORIOUS,
REGARDLESS OF MY PREDICAMENT.

Yea, though I walk through the valley of the shadow of death, I will fear no evil; for You are with me; Your rod and Your staff, they comfort me. (Psalm 23:4)

Lessons Unspoken

I lived in freedom while dying to my own will and embracing God's perfect will. Then, on May 25, 2009, I delivered a miracle, Lorelle Faith. I never imagined I would have such a journey of life, love, pain, healing, and loss. Right now, I honor my youngest daughter's life, a child who, never speaking a word, taught me how to live. My daughter's life was a testimony lived and a legacy remembered. Every time I think of her birthday, I smile because, that day, we were both birthed in different ways.

Some people cannot name the person God sent to change their life ultimately, but I carried, birthed, and buried my shero. Sometimes, I smile when I want to feel close to my daughter. I try to emulate her irreplaceable attributes so that my life may speak of her legacy.

How did your loved one make your life better? Does your grief give a glimpse into its impact on your life?

REMEMBER, UNSPOKEN WORDS ARE TRANSLATED BEAUTIFULLY THROUGH ACTIONS!

And we know that all things work together for good to those who love God, to those who are the called according to His purpose. (Romans 8:28)

Invisible Chain

Fear can constrain a person in more ways than one. Philippians 4:6 tells us not to be anxious about anything, but in every situation, by prayer and petition with thanksgiving, present your requests to God. I remember being so fearful and anxious when Lorelle was alive, fearful and anxious about seizures, potential sickness, and even death. I was so scared and nervous that I almost missed the chance to enjoy her life. Do not let what *could* happen rob you of the joys of the present moment.

Do you find yourself fearful and anxious? If you do, the time is now. It is the time to stop and pray, stop and believe, and know that God is Sovereign. God will keep you through everything that you face in this world. Death can bind us to our future, perception, peace, and hope. The key word is death *can*, but it *won't* with fervent prayer. Do not allow death to cause you to die while living.

We are free to feel and to live after loss!

Fear not, for I am with you; be not dismayed, for I am your God. I will strengthen you. Yes, I will help you; I will uphold you with My righteous right hand. (Isaiah 41:10)

Facing What I Can't Fake

My grief I had to face! I tried to be numb, run from it, sleep in it, and work through it, but grief found me. It wanted to consume me and suffocate me. My tears tried to drown me; my numbness wished to destroy me; my depression tried to oppress me; my heartache tried to kill me. I wanted to cover grief up with makeup and decrease it with laughter, but it appeared. I masked it, but the mask found a way to fall off. I tried to isolate it. My silent screams were spiritually audible. Grief relentlessly pursued my will to fight…and it almost won.

Grief is a skillful contender but not the champion. What happened every time? Well, GRIEF MET GOD! When grief met God, it had to bow! My God is not only skillful; He is my Savior! My God is a Way Maker! He is a Miracle Worker, a Promise Keeper, and a Light in the Darkness! MY GOD, that is Who You ARE!

REINTRODUCE GRIEF TO GOD, WHO HAS ALREADY CONQUERED DEATH!

The last enemy that will be destroyed is death.
(1 Corinthians 15:26)

DEFINE OKAY

If you are grieving the death of a loved one, it is okay not to be okay. However, it is vital to express your truth; losing someone is painful and does not feel okay. Grief does not follow a beautiful, perfect plan; it can come like a storm and reside like a squatter. It is not easy, but you can live with grief. The key is not to exist with grief, but to live with grief. When I chose to live my best life in honor of my daughter, just existing was no longer an option. Grief hurts, and everyone may not understand your agony. But God does. Grieving is normal, and you do not have to process it alone.

Whether you have lost someone suddenly, as we did, or if it was a gradual passing, no one can ever be completely ready for the moment of death. It aches deeply. Time does not heal all wounds. Many of us bear scars of sorrow, and together we can cope. You do not have to grieve alone!

MY OKAY IS DEFINED BY MY TRUTH!

Jesus wept. (John 11:35)

Revised Agenda

It is all right to turn down opportunities because your self-care matters. I have been encouraging everyone to practice self-care, but sadly I myself fell short. I thought I was a terrible person if I did not accept a ministry invite, because I love ministry, sharing the love of God, and being in fellowship. However, this season is different. God's ministry is a part of everything I do. I must learn to be okay with saying no so that I can say yes to God.

Personal reflection: On Monday, November 23, 2015, my daughter died at 5:30 a.m. as I lay under her feet. The weekend before she died, I was busy helping others and preparing for church events when the ministry was essentially in my house. That Sunday night before she died, I was exhausted because I could not balance myself. I had said yes to everyone and essentially no to God.

During my grieving, guess what? Programs continued, life continued, and I learned a painful lesson. You will go empty trying to keep others full. After my daughter died, I vowed not to preach or dance again, but the ministry wasn't the problem; my schedule and decisions caused exhaustion. BUT GOD showed me His Sovereignty, showed me how to take the time to fill myself up so that people get what is the best of me, and not just what is left of me.

Honor yourself in choosing you. Then fill up and pour out!

THE HOLY SPIRIT NOW SCHEDULES APPOINTMENTS!

However, when He, the Spirit of Truth, has come, He will guide you into all truth; for He will not speak on His own authority, but whatever He hears He will speak, and He will tell you things to come. (John 16:13)

IT Is So!

How do you rest in IT? I remember looking at multiple machines, trying to drown out the noise of the beeping ventilator, and praying for peace because of the prognosis given by the doctors. Somehow, Lorelle, hooked to the machines with the ventilator helping her breathe, IVs in her limbs, and pain patches for a wound on her foot, was still able to rest. God allowed her to rest in her affliction while she was healing. Somehow God blessed her with the ability to sleep while her body fought to stay alive. Her posture became my petition. I remember pleading with God to please show me how to rest in IT!

Honestly, I had FAITH, but no rest. So many sleepless nights, and I realized I had faith to do everything but rest. I was afraid to close my eyes because I thought I would miss something. Being Lorelle's mom during her life and death, I learned the true meaning of Hebrews 11:1. Now I see more with my eyes shut in faith than open in doubt. Daily, I work on resting in my faith. Why? Because in life, IT happens.

What is IT? For me, IT was being able to relax because I could not heal her. IT understands that I only have so much control over what happens in my life. IT is my accepting moments as they come. IT is not wishing away challenges, but learning in the process. IT is not praying for peace, but consciously working to be peaceful. IT is embracing the journey as it comes. IT is knowing my meekness is not a weakness. IT is falling in love with God repeatedly. IT is resting in the FACT that I serve The God who will give Rest in Unrest, Peace in Pain, Comfort in a Crisis, Healing to the Afflicted, and Grace in Grief. No matter what your IT is, trust God if He allows IT—He has a provision in IT.

WRITTEN WITHOUT CLIFFSNOTES
OR EDITING ENABLED.

But He answered and said, "It is written, 'Man shall not live by bread alone, but by every word that proceeds from the mouth of God.'" (Matthew 4:4)

ACCESS ALLOWED

Bereavement is a cave an individual can create if they choose. This cave can become a dark place where the entry appears open, but the exit is complicated. I formed a dwelling illuminated only by the light I chose to bring in. My sorrow was only as dark as I allowed it to be. Somehow I began to assume darkness equated to grief. So many people told me how to feel and what to feel I forgot to understand my feelings. Sadness rested in my sorrow, but memories of my loved one brought unspeakable joy. In the hope of healing my fragmented heart, I started to crave light in darkness, instead of simply allowing infinite illumination. I needed God to be a constant in my cave.

This acronym helps me in tough times: CAVE—Comfort Assurance Victory Everlasting. The Holy Spirit guides my comfort. My assurance is in the Word of God. My victory is in accepting that I will live beyond my sorrow. My everlasting hope will sustain me for a lifetime. The cave that could have become my isolation became my haven.

Remember, you have access to God, Who will not withhold His love from you, no matter how challenging your moment is.

BE THE LIGHT THAT ILLUMINATES YOUR DARKEST HOUR!

I have come as a light into the world, that whoever believes in Me should not abide in darkness. (John 12:46)

Upon a Star

Reflecting on my loss, I have one wish. I wish I'd had another day to hold you, rock you to sleep, and carry you in my arms. I wish I'd had time to share my unending love, hopes, and dreams with you. I wish you'd meet me in moments when I long to feel the softness of your hair and the peace in your presence. I wish I did not have to have tomorrows without you. I wish that stars were tangible and your heartbeat were palpable.

If Heaven had a phone, I would tell you for hours, days, and years how much I miss you. Instead, I search through hundreds of pictures, ensuring I always remember a moment you graced our life. Grief is no longer a place I visit; it has become where I find your legacy of love. Grief is persistent, yet not infinite. My love is more potent than sorrow. My mourning heart has roots that grow beyond the grave. I am unapologetically allowing grief to be part of my story, but not its title. When the day you wish for never comes, can you find joy in the days that have passed?

WILLING TO WISH WHILE DARING TO DREAM!

I would have lost heart, unless I had believed that I would see the goodness of the Lord in the land of the living. (Psalm 27:13)

No Vacancies

L ove is what you were and what you left. My daughter will forever be one of the most beautiful parts of my past, present, and future. Since I cannot change reality, I find peace in the past. I read a post by an unknown author; it said, "The past is a place of reference and not a place of residence." If your past is full of joy, let it be a place of rejuvenation. If your past reminds you of a loved one's life, let it be a place of remembrance. If your past was complicated, let it be a place of replenishing, and when it is a place of grief, let it be a place of restoration. Most importantly, let your residence be in the Rest of God when the past tries to influence your responses negatively.

We acknowledge our past. It is unnecessary to forget your past because our history holds lessons and love that shape who we are. Let us remember our yesterdays, be grateful for today and strengthened for tomorrow.

THERE IS A FUTURE WITHIN
THIS SPECIFIC JOURNEY.

He who dwells in the secret place of the Most High shall abide under the shadow of the Almighty. (Psalm 91:1)

CAN YOU STOP?

STOP! Stop rushing time! Stop showing up but not being present! Stop focusing only on what is to come and not being thankful for what is here! Stop thinking about tomorrow to the extent that you don't enjoy today!

God keeps reminding me to stop. Why change my focus from planning and preparing for next week, month, and year? God whispered, "Because you are planning, but missing the beauty in today." He reminded me of Jeremiah 29:11: "For I know the thoughts that I think toward you, says the Lord, thoughts of peace and not of evil, to give you a future and a hope."

God clearly showed me that I must remember the Lord's Prayer, which tells me to ask Him for my daily bread. I share this because we often put things that matter on hold or rush conversations or moments that soon become memories. We are confident in tomorrow when God has given us so much beauty and time today!

Remember to call someone, connect, hug, smile, and thank God for the daily bread of this day. Tomorrow will soon become today. Lorelle's death taught me a painful lesson that tomorrow does not always come, so be grateful for today's blessing! No matter how much I planned for tomorrow, I could not hold on to her today.

I PRAY THAT WE ALL STOP (SHARE, TALK, OVERCOME, AND PRAY) DAILY.

Therefore do not worry about tomorrow, for tomorrow will worry about its own things. Sufficient for the day is its own trouble. (Matthew 6:34)

Dear God,

As believers, we declare the good news: "For unto us a Child is born, unto us a Son is given, and the government will be upon His shoulder. And His name will be called Wonderful, Counselor, Mighty God, Everlasting Father, Prince of Peace" (Isaiah 9:6). Your peace surpasses our understanding and helps to strengthen our stance, empower our voices, and ensure our faith. I have loved You with everlasting love and affection. My Lord, You have never been anything but my source of living. The truth is all You can accept, so I freely give it to You.

On the day Lorelle died, I was devastated. I had faithfully accepted her diagnosis, prognosis, and challenges, but her death was a different story. My prayer was to let her live. When she died, I could not even thank You for the time we had because I was mourning a future we would not have. God, I was so broken. You fired me from my favorite job, took my love, and shifted my ministry. I could not understand why because I only desired to be a mom to all my kids.

In her death, I became another type of Mom, a bereaved one. Lorelle died right before my eyes. She flatlined, You took Your breath back, and I felt as if You'd taken mine too. She died, and I was struggling to live. I wanted to be mad, I tried to blame You, but I revered You as the giver and taker of life. Honestly, I found no fault in You, God. I just wanted a different outcome.

You made me not only a reciter of the Scriptures, but I had to be a living scripture in this loss. You sustained me, kept me, hid me, strengthened me, loved me, held me, and did everything I needed and more. Thank You for never leaving me. Thank You, God, for the written and living Word. I could not have made it a second without Your grace.

I had never felt such a stripping and unbearable separation before the loss of my child. I searched the Scriptures for solace and remembered Mary, Jesus's mother. Mary experienced the loss of a child, yet You still called her blessed. For that reason, I do not feel pitiful, even in sorrow. I carry her ability to live in my heart. Just think, Mary lost not only her son, but our Savior. I cannot imagine the pain she felt. We bless God that Jesus was the resurrected promise of an eternal life.

When I recall her transition, God, I am grateful to have been a witness. God, You watched Your only begotten Son die a human death, so who am I to be exempt? God, my heart still aches, and weeping comes even in joy. I appreciate Your considering me for this journey because I found more of You after losing my daughter. Thank You for allowing my daughter eternal rest until we meet again. Her life was not in vain, and my shattered heart will continue to mend. Thank You for leaving the Holy Spirit, Who comforts without ceasing.

Tearful thanksgiving,
Lorelle's Mommy

HEALING OR JUST DEALING

Just because you are healing from something doesn't mean you don't have to deal with the residue. When my wounds heal, I still have a scar. The scar reminds me that something happened; I want to acknowledge what it was or was not. When someone passes, loved ones carry invisible scars. Unfortunately, we do not attend to what is not visible, which leads to the grieving individual feeling forgotten.

Have you ever felt alone in a room full of people? The fact that sorrow does not have a specific look does not negate its existence.

I do not know how you feel about losing a loved one, but I am praying for you. We all experience loss differently and yet the same. It is agonizing. Being full of FAITH does not make you exempt from feeling it. Do not aim to become numb. God can heal what you feel!

God will comfort you. Please hold on to God if you feel as if you are suffocating in your pain. Faithfully, I have prayed, cried, been quiet, fasted, and had a grief counselor. I finally understand what my grandparents said: "God is a resting place." If you are grieving, know you are not forgotten or alone. You can unapologetically grieve in grace.

THE GOD OF YOUR GRIEF IS THE SAME GOD OF YOUR GRACE!

My flesh and my heart fail, but God is the strength of my heart and my portion forever. (Psalm 73:26)

Unfathomable Yet Palpable

A parent's grief is unexplainable and, at times, inconsolable when a child dies. After my daughter died, I learned that we all grieve differently. Suffering happens without death. I watched my parents grieve for me because they could not stop my pain. It made me reflect on all the times I saw them worry about me as they watched me develop and deal with the trials and tribulations in life. I never comprehended until I had my children how deeply you can hurt when your children hurt. Pain in a parent's heart is not only felt in death.

Every time Lorelle had a seizure or needed resuscitation, a piece of my heart broke. I spent much time profoundly grieving my living child, instead of rejoicing in her life. I wish sometimes I had learned to celebrate her presence without worrying about her prognosis. Now that she is gone, I am attempting to parent differently by enjoying the moments and not rushing my children's process of growing up.

My perspective has changed, and I turned my challenges into blessings. I am not anxious for tomorrow; I am focusing on unpacking every opportunity of every day with gratitude.

GOD'S DAILY BREAD SATISFIES
ME REGARDLESS OF THE PORTION.

*Let, I pray, Your merciful kindness be for my comfort,
according to Your word to Your servant.* (Psalm 119:76)

A Parent's Petition

Gracious grief was vital for my other children. I want to encourage other parents secretly grieving situations and issues with their living children. For some of us, parenting is not always easy! Some of us are grieving the plans for our children, grieving relationships we want with our children, grieving health issues in our children, and even grieving past dreams we had for our children. Perhaps your child is dealing with drugs, alcoholism, mental illness, domestic abuse, incarceration, bullying, or any other tricky thing that life can bring. Still, you must hold on. Be encouraged, parents, and do not stop praying. If you need to repent for something you did or did not do, repent, forgive yourself, and do better. Do not let the guilt of the past control your gain in the future. God can redeem the past.

If you did your best but still feel as if your child's struggle is your own, remember it is not your battle; it is the Lord's. Do not be afraid to ask God for wisdom. Seek a support system, and cast your burdens on the Lord. Remember, your children are God's children first, and He cares for them too. God is the best parent we can have. If you have children still living, DO NOT LET YOUR GRIEF OVERSHADOW YOUR BELIEF! God will allow you to trust Him in your child's process. It does not matter if your child is five or fifty-five; you, as their parent, can still pray for their total healing.

THE HEALING PROCESS DOES
NOT HAVE AN EXPIRATION DATE.

*Casting all your care upon Him, for
He cares for you.* (1 Peter 5:7)

MAY GOD REMEMBER

There is a month highly personal to me. May is the fifth month, and five is the biblical number of grace. May is a month when "May flowers are supposed to grow." May is the month of Mother's Day. May is the month of Lorelle's birthday. May is the month, I learned, of Bereaved Mother's Day. A day set aside for a group of mothers who have lost children naturally, but carry them very much alive in their hearts.

I often close my eyes to remember my baby girl—the way she smelled, the touch of her hair, and the beauty in her smile. I rejoice in the memory of when people knew I was a mom of four, not three, and of caring for a miracle who knew only how to endure with a smile. At times, I close my eyes when tears cloud my visions of our unforgettable six years together. In this profound time of reflection, I beg God to endow me with His love, comfort, and grace. Endow means "to give, to provide, to make able."

I am simply sharing this because, sometimes, we can be transparent with joy, but unable to share the inner cry. God always answers my inner cry because He is a consistent helper for His children. The answer, I learned, does not stop the utterance; it merely reminds me that nothing I pray is in vain. The same God Who kept my daughter will keep you and me. Maybe you have not lost a child—I pray you never do—but whatever your heart grieves, be encouraged that God is nearby.

Ask God to ENDOW you with whatever you require during your prayer time. He is more than able. I pray "May" God be glorified even in how I grieve. My grieving is my eternal love for my daughter expressed from a heart I buried her memory within!

MAY YOU REJOICE THAT YOUR
PRAYERS ARE NOT FORGOTTEN.

Trust in the Lord with all your heart, and lean not on your own understanding. (Proverbs 3:5)

Sweet Surrender

G IVE UP! I DID; I HAD TO. I finally had to GIVE UP, leaning on my understanding. I had to GIVE UP my agenda, GIVE UP trying to figure it all out, GIVE UP trying to help God write what is already written, GIVE UP complaining, GIVE UP stressing, GIVE UP failing, and GIVE UP worrying.

WHY? Because I only want to GIVE UP TO GOD, WHO CAN HANDLE IT. THEREFORE, I GIVE UP PRAISE, GIVE UP WORSHIP, GIVE UP THANKS-GIVING TO GOD, FOR HE IS ABLE, AMAZING, ALL-KNOWING, AND ALL GOOD!

SOMETIMES LOVE IS IN LETTING GO.

The Lord is my rock and my fortress and my deliverer; my God, my strength, in whom I will trust; my shield and the horn of my salvation, my stronghold. (Psalm 18:2)

THE WILL IN HIS WILL

It is hard for me to accept His perfect will when it hurts. Disappointments and heartaches have tested my faith in areas I thought were solidified. I had no idea that I had begun to diminish God in my difficulty, quantifying His blessings.

Personally, in sorrow, I started only to ask God the minimum: Why? Not because I questioned His ability, but, honestly, I was just grateful for whatever God did in my life. I had dealt with so many ups and downs that I had begun to be satisfied with just breathing, with no phone calls about tragedies, and with the fact that I serve a Sovereign God.

I realize now I had placed limits on my expectations of how God would reign in all facets of my life. Did I feel unworthy? Had I found peace in what I had and did not want to ask for more? Well, it was a combination of a lot of emotions. God is great and phenomenal, and I feared being selfish. However, God wanted me to pray for HIS will in my life. Why? His will is perfect, and all things concerning me and assigned for me are all tucked into His will for my life.

I want to encourage someone who is just existing, not living, in the fullness of God. God has a Will for your life. He Will take care of you. He Will come through for you. He Will provide for you. He Will heal you. He Will deliver you. He Will do all things but fail for you.

GOD WILL ALLOW TESTING AND BLESSINGS.

> *From the end of the Earth I will cry to You*
> *when my heart is overwhelmed; lead me to*
> *the rock that is higher than I.* (Psalm 61:2)

The Answer

God has the final say. God still works miracles. You don't always have to be correct, but try to be righteous. Do not be afraid to call old friends and spend time with loved ones. Know that depression and anxiety can cease, and terminal illnesses be cured. Your life is good, and challenging times are not in vain. You can live again. Be the best you can manage and don't apologize; there is strength in letting go. Never forget there is also wisdom in holding on; you can try again, you can love again, you can trust again, and you can heal again. You can enjoy the journey—including the hills, bumps, and valleys—and finally live a life to be remembered. Be present now; do not assume you have later or tomorrow.

The response for today may carry you for tomorrow.

And the Lord, He is the One who goes before you. He will be with you; He will not leave you nor forsake you. Do not fear nor be dismayed. (Deuteronomy 31:8)

In an Instant

Sudden death can knock the wind out of your lungs and cause you to gasp for air while suffocating in quicksand. It can feel as if time is standing still in the middle of darkness, the nightmare of a valley of despair and sadness. Sudden death seems so cruel and relentless. One minute a person is there, and the next they are gone. Sudden death is no respecter of time, place, or feeling. It just comes. It waits for no last-minute conversation, last hugs, final words, or one last "I love you." Sudden death is just that—sudden.

When I suddenly lost Lorelle, it opened my eyes to the grief people experience when death comes without warning. I think about my patients at work; one day, they may be smiling and doing well, and, the next day, they have passed. Honestly, I started to live anxiously, afraid of "sudden death." I did not know how to live without expecting a tragedy, without preparing for the next blow. I found I was not living; I was existing. So I prayed and asked God for insight on what I could learn from my experience, from the grief I felt for loved ones who had suddenly died.

God in His word reminded me that He is the author and finisher of our faith, the Alpha and Omega. Death did not take God by surprise. That was my comfort—I served a God Who still had power over death and provided for my loved ones.

Please know that, even though I do not doubt Him, the pain is still real, but there is a lesson in all things. I want to share what Sudden Death has taught me: love unconditionally; forgive without end; cherish every second; do not just plan your life—live your plan; smile just because; do not go to bed mad; stop holding grudges; speak the truth in love; kindness still wins; and hope remains.

APPRECIATION FOR THE TIME BESTOWED.

And you would be secure because there is hope; yes, you would dig around you and take your rest in safety. (Job 11:18)

Now What?

Not having new memories is one of the most painful parts of losing a loved one. It is living in the present, but always trying to hold on to the past while anticipating the future. Today is a reality of yesterday's memories, which are full of people and things still sorely missed and tomorrows that will never come. Live life with a legacy and love, in a way that the very thought of you makes those who remain cry with a smile. When I close my eyes, I remember you and me; I remember us.

It is Who you miss.

You number my wanderings, put my tears into Your bottle. Are they not in Your book? (Psalm 56:8)

SCARRED SORROW

Wounds are painful, and sometimes the healing can be excruciating. Wounds sometimes are easier to cover up, but often must be exposed to air in order to heal. When we pray for Total Healing, it is Holistic. Losing a loved one is complex and does not end with a eulogy. Take time today to recognize someone's wounds; if you cannot help, don't hurt. Wounds can be addressed with love, listening, and compassion. Honestly, you can cause more damage by carelessly ripping off the scab or abrasively washing a wound. Not every wound requires the same healing regimen. When a wound is exposed, it may bleed, but that is a sign often that blood is still flowing to that area, simply because it is still viable.

Just because someone is still crying and grieving does not mean they are prolonging the process. Let it signify that they are still feeling, which is often better than being numb. Stay encouraged that, whatever your wound is, You CAN BE HEALED. MAY GOD TOUCH AND HEAL EVERY WOUND, THOSE EXPOSED AND THOSE HIDDEN!

SMILE AND KEEP THE F.A.I.T.H.
GOD IS A HEALER!

*He heals the brokenhearted and binds
up their wounds.* (Psalm 147:3)

You Live

S ometimes you must stop and look your blessing in the face, eye to eye, and trust God enough to say, "Lord, I'm ready!" Ready to live and not just exist; to do His Will, His Way; and to let Him be Sovereign in every area of your life. If something is hindering you, burdening you, or keeping you down, Have FAITH to see grace in those people viewed as broken. Some saw disability; we Saw God's ABILITY!

You will make it!

O Lord, You have pleaded the case for my soul;
You have redeemed my life. (Lamentations 3:58)

Abled Affliction

We face many deaths and challenges, but GOD IS STILL SOVEREIGN. I remember being devastated that my daughter died…until I began to celebrate that she lived. Grief took a lot from me, but I refused to give it my joy. Daily, I pray for Grace over Grief. Lord, as we prepare for the holidays, celebrations, milestones, and just life, I ask You to please fill our emptiness. We know You are able—please be willing!

My ability to rejoice is intertwined with my promise to remember.

Be strong and of good courage; do not fear nor be afraid of them; for the Lord your God, He is the One who goes with you. He will not leave you nor forsake you. (Deuteronomy 31:6)

THOSE WHO REMAIN

We walk among you
We sit among you

We pray among you

We work among you

We talk with you

We sing with you

We eat with you

We are everywhere and nowhere at the same time

We are present and daydreaming at the same time

We are rejoicing and grieving at the same time

We are whole and empty at the same time

We are parents who have lost a child

We are parents who are not alone

We are parents who have a heart with a wound

We are full of strength that can carry

We are living in the legacies of the children we buried.

Hug someone; you never know if they could be part of the WE!

WHEN YOUR CHILD HAS NO MORE TOMORROWS,
ALL YOU HAVE ARE YESTERDAYS!

Blessed are those who mourn, for
they shall be comforted. (Matthew 5:4)

PRESENT HELP

There is a time for everything! I had a beautiful conversation with a grieving mother, which made me reflect on losing a child and a loved one. As a Christian, I thought I initially had to mourn peacefully and be OKAY. However, I am anchored in knowing God did not say I had to be OKAY with losing my daughter. The Bible says in 1 Thessalonians 4:13-14, "But I do not want you to be ignorant, brethren, concerning those who have fallen asleep, lest you sorrow as others who have no hope. For if we believe that Jesus died and rose again, even so God will bring with Him those who sleep in Jesus." This verse reminds me to GRIEVE WITH HOPE, BUT IT DOES SAY WITHOUT HURT! I hurt and grieve, and NONE OF THAT SHIFTS WHAT I BELIEVE!

Do not let anyone define your grief! I have learned to be unapologetically human with FAITH! I need God; I petition and praise Him, and I am nothing without Him. He can only accept my truth. My truth is that I cannot make it without HIM. God has reminded me that I am not His sidekick or superhuman; I am His daughter. So when I tell God, "I need Your Comfort," He whispers, "I am here."

Pray for people who say they are okay, but the truth is that they are not. This message is to free the grieving, depressed, sad, brokenhearted, disappointed, or angry person living in "okayness." Be so unrestricted as to Live

during it ALL, for the Joy of the Lord is your strength.
God does not run out of JOY—tell Him what you need.
HE IS LISTENING!

THE HELP WE NEED COMES FROM THE
ONE WHO DOES NOT NEED HELP!

*Now may the God of hope fill you with all joy and
peace in believing, that you may abound in hope by
the power of the Holy Spirit.* (Romans 15:13)

ABOVE ME

The phrase "It is above me" now rings in my ear. All my heartaches, petitions, and sorrows are above me. I take comfort in knowing that God sits high and looks low. Low is a position that I have assumed in bereavement. Low and lowly is where I find solace under my Mighty and Big God. Under God, I can hand Him what I cannot carry. I am in a position to be picked up and no longer let down. In the posture of prayer, God finds me awaiting His power to lift and withstand. The knowledge of where God is assists me in being steadfast in the reality of life. As I repeat the serenity prayer, I accept and exchange. I accept what God gives and what He keeps from me. I trade my understanding for His peace. The weight of my worry and my sorrow had become crushing. God took what crushed me and replaced it with comfort.

I HAVE THAT TOO — GOD

Though the Lord is on high, yet He regards the lowly, but the proud He knows from afar. (Psalm 138:6)

DEAR GRIEF

The reason I am writing to you is to expose you. Yes, you are necessary and have your agenda—I get it. You do not exist to some, but you are extremely familiar to me. However, there is an issue I must address. You are part of my life, but have less power than you think. I indeed welcomed you after several losses in my life, especially my daughter Lorelle, but you have things attached to you that are not welcome.

Understand, Grief, you came into my life, but, soon after, you invited depression, suicidal thoughts, anxiety, devastation, and worthlessness. For a minute, I entertained your guests, but then I remembered this is my house, God's sanctuary, and they are no longer welcome where He abides. Frankly, all your guests have to go because I have let them overstay their welcome. Grief, I know you enter and leave, and that's okay because I will never stop missing all I lost, but it does not compare to what I have gained.

I gained grace in your place, and grace is not only sufficient, but also consistent. Grief, I know you did not invite them formally, but they came anyway. Let's not digress. Guess what? Grief, when depression, suicidal thoughts, anxiety, devastation, and worthlessness leave, Grace's Friends will come. Grace brings Peace, Unspeakable Joy, Abundant Life, Self-Worth, and even Faith. So, Grief, I know our relationship is not over, but it is different because Grace's Friends will be Residents. I am comfortable in my skin, and my house will be a home in which I can abide in the secret place of the Most High.

Unapologetically,

THE BEREAVED BELIEVER

REFLECTIONS

The author has skillfully and creatively woven together her experience with grief and belief in God to clarify why she is a Bereaved Believer. Any person who has grieved the loss of a loved one will find comfort in knowing that you're not alone. Your feelings and emotions may vacillate and change over time, and it's okay never to stop missing your loved one. I rejoice knowing I witnessed and was a partaker in the author's journey as Lorelle's grandmother, without realizing the depth and unwanted guests that sometimes accompany grief. I thank God for His Grace and Mercies that renew daily. God Bless you, Kodi, for truthfully sharing your journey as a Bereaved Believer. May this book bless many who have experienced, or are experiencing grief, as it has blessed me.

—Gail Dolman-Smith

When Kodi asked if I would provide a testimonial of her draft devotional manuscript, I was honored to be considered someone who gets the opportunity to go on a journey with her. However, when I learned her book was about grief, I told myself I shouldn't take this journey, mainly since I had lost a son. But I knew she would write a book that would be spiritual, vulnerable, and unapologetic. In this book, Kodi touches the heart like an EKG and records the grieving symptoms related to heart problems. Then, she performs a heart surgery using scriptures that remove grieving scars that damage the heart. She gets you on a spiritual path that causes you to rest in God and dwell in the secret place of the Most High, where she, Kodi, abides under the shadow of the Almighty!

—Dorothy Watkins

B eing a mother without a child was the worst feeling I have ever had. On my first Mother's Day, May 8th, my only child had just left me three days earlier. My body ached, and my arms and heart felt like lead; they were empty. I was empty. I like the saying, "When you don't know what to do, just pray." I remember when my daughter was first diagnosed, and my sister reminded me of this.

"What good will that do? It's terminal," I responded, defeated.

"Well, it can't hurt" was her response.

If any of you lacks wisdom, let him ask of God,
who gives to all liberally and without reproach,
and it will be given to him. (James 1:5)

Praying was the only thing I could do in desperation and defeat. Though I did not know what power it could have, I kept at it. Prayer could not change my daughter's diagnosis. I had to realize that I was not praying for a miracle but for strength and my survival. Twelve years later, it has helped me to endure her loss and become who I am today: stronger, wiser, and more resilient.

For those who don't believe in prayer, remember that it is good to be sad about sad things. Carry your sorrow for as long as you need to, and then allow yourself to put it down. Seek help from those who offer. Rest when you are weary. I once thought that if I wasn't grieving, I was forgetting about her. Now I am no longer sorrowful, but

I still carry her everywhere I go. This is because fetal cells migrate into the mother's body during pregnancy. So every child you carry becomes a part of you forever.

I have known Kodi Pride since we were ten years old. We shared a lot then, mostly laughter. We never knew we would share this cross as mothers. Reading this manuscript reminded me how difficult it is for some people to understand how to react when they lose a child, but those who share the experience understand something so profound. There is an unspoken sisterhood, a bond, an invisible string that ties us together. While the connection is precious, I do not wish it upon anyone else. Let us continue to support mothers in pain and need. Kodi has written a beautiful testimony to her endless journey.

Sincerely,
Meg Smith Aeschliman
—Mother of Maria Grace Aeschliman, May 5, 2011

K odi Pride is unapologetically naked in this book as she gives the reader access to her aggrieved heart and soul in the loss of her daughter. No filter. A loss in which she gained divine insight and wisdom as to how the living should LIVE! I read each passage with her words jumping off the page and right into my heart. Challenging me to internalize spiritually what it really means to experience the grace of God and how daily gratitude positions us to receive His peace fully. Kodi's transparency leaves no room for ambiguity on how her daughter's life blessed her and how her death transformed her. What a powerful testimony layered with a mother's love for her child and her unconditional love for Her God. It's authentic. It's honest. It's what I've always known Kodi to be...real!

—Danita Harris

Reading through the chronicles of your experiences took me on the intimate journey of profound loss into spaces of overwhelming isolation and desperation that led to resurrection into a welcomed and deep dependency that led to a fortified unwavering faith! Faith that says "Though He slay me, yet will I trust Him" (Job 13:15).

We are His children, and every hurt, every loss, every triumph, and every victory is shared with and belongs to Him too! In our weakness, HE is strong! The soil of loss has been the fertilizer to your faith. Thank God He looks beyond not only our masks but also our walls! He came in and loved you back to life, like the loving Father He is.

Grief is a spirit that can sometimes become a stronghold. Your ultimate surrender to His will opened up your designated path to walk in victory. You were called to this journey, anointed for this purpose and unwanted pain. I only share in your loss to a certain degree, and I've never experienced such profound pain that took my breath away. But God!

We were blessed to have such amazing pure love and light in our lives, an awesome angel that gave hugs that felt like heaven! However, I would not exchange the blessing of Lorelle to avoid the pain of the loss. She enriched my life probably more than I did hers (or at least as much) without uttering a single word. She was the epitome of actions that speak louder than words! So to a small degree, I understand your journey.

The insights and transparency of your trials you have penned here are a legacy that will live on well past our time on Earth. Thank you for sharing how great our God is and how unfailing His love is for His children.

—Mersula Franklin

READER'S PERSONAL REFLECTION

About the Author

K **odi B. Pride** is a multifaceted woman dedicated to family, inspired by dreamers, molded by challenges, and refined by God. She is married with four children, three living and one transitioned. She is an occupational therapist, a federal contractor, a licensed minister, the founder of the Lorelle F.A.I.T.H. Foundation, a ghost-writer, and a consistent backer of numerous entities in ministry and advocacy. Yet Kodi's most profound achievements are embedded in her testimonies, not her resume. Her mission is to live a life that exemplifies the statement, "Who I am represents Whose I am!" Ministry is her life, and she is dancing her way through it.